Dear Parent:
Your child's love of reading starts here!

Every child learns to read in a different way and at his or her own speed. Some go back and forth between reading levels and read favorite books again and again. Others read through each level in order. You can help your young reader improve and become more confident by encouraging his or her own interests and abilities. From books your child reads with you to the first books he or she reads alone, there are I Can Read Books for every stage of reading:

SHARED READING
Basic language, word repetition, and whimsical illustrations, ideal for sharing with your emergent reader

BEGINNING READING
Short sentences, familiar words, and simple concepts for children eager to read on their own

READING WITH HELP
Engaging stories, longer sentences, and language play for developing readers

READING ALONE
Complex plots, challenging vocabulary, and high-interest topics for the independent reader

ADVANCED READING
Short paragraphs, chapters, and exciting themes for the perfect bridge to chapter books

I Can Read Books have introduced children to the joy of reading since 1957. Featuring award-winning authors and illustrators and a fabulous cast of beloved characters, I Can Read Books set the standard for beginning readers.

A lifetime of discovery begins with the magical words **"I Can Read!"**

Visit www.icanread.com for information
on enriching your child's reading experience.

I Can Read Book® is a trademark of HarperCollins Publishers.

Library of Congress Control Number: 2015938894
ISBN 978-0-06-230389-9 (trade bdg.)—978-0-06-230388-2 (pbk.)

Pete the Cat
SCUBA-CAT

by James Dean

HARPER
An Imprint of HarperCollinsPublishers

Pete the Cat is excited.

He is going scuba diving!

Pete puts on a mask and fins.

He has a tank full of air.

He hopes to see lots of fish.

"If you are lucky,

you might see a seahorse,"

says Captain Joe.

"A seahorse?" says Pete.

"I can't wait!

I never saw one before."

"Their ridges look like
a horse's mane,"
says Captain Joe.

"Groovy," says Pete.

Pete jumps into the water.

Splash!

Down, down, down he goes.

Up, up, up go the bubbles.

Pete looks for a seahorse.

He sees a swordfish.

Pete swims out of its way.

Pete waves to a stingray.

It has a long, skinny tail.

That's not a seahorse,

thinks Pete.

Pete looks high and low

for the seahorse.

Then he feels a tickle.

Pete sees a school of fish.

They all look alike.

Except for one.

It puffs up.

It is a blowfish!

It is not a seahorse.

Where could one be?

Pete looks in the rocks.

What is that?

It is an octopus!

It has eight legs.

It is not a seahorse.

Pete feels a tickle.

What could it be?

18

Pete turns.

He sees a cave!

Is there a seahorse inside?

Pete sees a crab with claws.

A seahorse does not have claws,

Pete thinks.

The cave is getting darker.

Pete feels a tickle.

Then he sees an eel!

Pete swims past it.

It is too long to be a seahorse.

Oh no! It is too dark to see!

How will Pete get out?

Pete sees a jellyfish.

It glows in the dark.

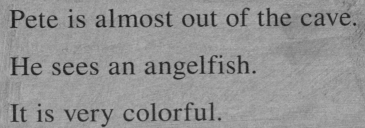

Pete is almost out of the cave.

He sees an angelfish.

It is very colorful.

Pete is out of the cave.

So why is it so dark?

Pete is in a shadow. . . .

He is in the shadow
of a whale!
Yikes!

Pete wishes he could jump on
a seahorse and ride away!

Pete hops on a sea turtle instead.

It takes him to the boat.

I did not see a seahorse,

thinks Pete.

He feels a tickle on his tail.

"A seahorse!" cries Pete.

"What a surprise!"

"You were with me all along!"

says Pete.

"What a cool adventure!"